All Is Calm

All Is Calm

REFLECTIONS FOR ADVENT AND OTHER BUSY SEASONS

by Donna Schaper

SAINT MARY'S PRESS
CHRISTIAN BROTHERS PUBLICATIONS
WINONA, MINNESOTA

Genuine recycled paper with 10% post-consumer waste.
Printed with soy-based ink.

The publishing team included Michael Wilt, development editor;
Rebecca Fairbank, manuscript editor; Stephan Nagel, cover de-
signer; pre-press, printing, and binding by the graphics division
of Saint Mary's Press.

Cover painting by Charles Perkalis.

The scriptural quotations herein are from the New Revised Standard
Version of the Bible. Copyright ©1989 by the Division of Christian
Education of the National Council of the Churches of Christ in the
United States of America.

The quote by Susan Sontag on page 16 is reprinted from *The Writer's
Desk*, by Jill Krementz (New York: Random House, 1996), page 17.
Copyright ©1996 by Jill Krementz.

   The quote by William Shakespeare on page 43 is from *The Rape of
Lucrece*, line 939, and the quote by William Blake on page 67 is the
opening stanza of the poem "Auguries of Innocence." Both are
quoted from *The Oxford Dictionary of Quotations*, fourth edition, edited
by Angela Partington (New York: Oxford University Press, 1992),
pages 632 and 110. Copyright ©1992 by Oxford University Press.

   The quotes by Rainer Maria Rilke on pages 54 and 58 (from *The
Workman's Letter*) and the quotes by Kathleen Norris on pages 54–55
are from *Amazing Grace: A Vocabulary of Faith*, by Kathleen Norris (New
York: Riverhead Books, a division of Penguin Putnam, 1998), pages
161, 162, and 291, respectively. Copyright ©1998 by Kathleen
Norris.

Printed in the United States of America

Printing: 9 8 7 6 5 4 3 2 1

Year: 2007 06 05 04 03 02 01 00 99

ISBN 0-88489-604-8

Contents

Introduction 1

One Day at a Time 5

Baggage 9

Calm Manages the Heavy Lifting 11

Calm Is a Promise of Renewal 13

The Calm of Clear Attention 15

Calm As Friends 19

Calm As Prayer 21

Calm As Inclusion 25

Zenny Calm 29

How Much Calm Is Enough? 31

Calm As a Consumer 33

Sometimes We Just Have to
Get Out of Our Own Way 39

Calm Waits for the Truth 41

Calm Families 45

Calm Quits and Revives 49

Calm Near, Calm Far Away 53

Calm Is Focus 57

Calm Is Tuning 61

Calm Is Fragments 63

Calm Is Magnification 67

Calm After Clutter 69

Traveling Light in the Grand Canyon 71

Calm in Trouble 75

Calm Is the Christmas Point of View 79

Go to Bethlehem 83

Introduction

ADVENT IS ALL ABOUT WAITING – AND waiting is one of the least calm things we do. My children can live five years in one two-hour car trip. We have mercifully developed a round entitled "When Are We Going to Get There?" One of the children starts it, a second chimes in, the third chimes in, and my husband and I finish it. The round only distracts us for three miles or so, assuming the cruise control is set on seventy miles per hour. But it gives us a good joke, and humor makes art of waiting as well as anything else.

Children are not alone in impatience. Most adults have similar bits on which they chomp: Friday afternoons on the job that seem like forever; a nurse's twelve-hour shift experienced as eleven hours too long; the wait for the car to be paid off, for that first month with one less check to write; waiting for the pot to boil.

The folk advice that a watched pot never boils is as useful as humor: wait, don't watch.

Advent's glorification of waiting is up against a tough audience. We tend not to like even the *idea* of waiting. "Now!" is our middle name.

How dare Advent challenge this audience to imagine the coming of a time when all will be calm. It requires more than humor and more than folk wisdom. Advent tames the anxiety of waiting with a promise as deep as the keel on a large sailboat. Advent promises Jesus Christ, and Jesus is the deep calm of holy nights and holy days.

This promise calms our voyages. It lets us go slow amid anxiety and fear about "when are we gonna get there." Advent loosens our clenched hands, our tapping fingers, our cruise's control. We make clear passage to the promised Christ.

This small collection of Advent reflections is a step-by-step loosening. It is a calming. It is folksy enough: wait, don't watch. Patience is not my virtue, as I have said a thousand times. Here I try to learn what I don't know.

All is calm. But most of us don't see the calm yet. What we see instead is the long list of holiday preparations: more stuff to buy, more lines to stand in, more obligations to meet. We see the *more* of obligation rather than the *less* of grace.

We have to look deeper. It may take us more than one season or one Advent discipline. But calm, through Christ, is a place at which we can arrive.

In any season.

We may even be there already and do not know it.

One Day at a Time

SAUL BELLOW, THE GREAT NOVELIST, ONCE remarked that writing a novel is similar to driving a car. He said that all we can see in night driving is what is in our headlights. Beyond that, we cannot see. The same thing, said Bellow, is true of writing a novel. We have to work with what we know in the present moment.

The worst thing about most of us is that we want to be calm *right now*. We are in a grave hurry to arrive at the spiritual place we think we ought to be. We want instant calm, when calm is by its very nature a slowing into something deeper than the frenzy of the moment.

I'll never forget a businessman screaming at an airline clerk during one of the big snowstorms last winter: "But you don't understand,

I *have* to get to New York *tonight.*" "No, you
don't," the clerk replied.

I want to give this man his due. I have also
felt that I had to be somewhere *tonight.* I imagine he was about to lose a lot of money or a
lot of fun, or to disappoint an already disappointed family, or all three. He was taking a hit.
His anxiety and frustration about his inter-
rupted journey may have been fully justified.
He had a real, not an imagined, problem.

The airline clerk was nevertheless spiritually
more savvy. "No, you don't." You do not have
to do all that you think you have to do. You
may allow time and space and weather their
due. You may float. You may let go of circumstances beyond your control. You don't have to
be happy about them so much as to recognize
them and live within them. We have to dive
deep where we are, slowly, and stick to what
we can see in our headlights. We will likely be
surprised by just how much there is to see and
feel and experience wherever we are.

When this man calms down, he may even
enjoy a good novel. Or make a new friend. Or
have a good laugh at the unpredictability of his
otherwise perfectly controlled life.

In crowded airports on stormy nights, we see as much calm as we see anxiety. Some experienced travelers do their best work during such unplanned adventures. Some have their best fun. I remember sitting on the laps of two other people sitting on a lap in a van driving us all to the last flight out of Columbus. Our commuter adventure was marked by memorable laughter. Hotels fill up when people are stranded. Some people actually have parties in the lobbies. Commuting turns from drudgery to dancing. Not everyone can dance. Calm comes to those who can.

Calm is something we may or may not know today. It is not something we will always know. What we see in today's headlights always has the potential to bring calm.

Advent's trick is this: Jesus is not only coming. Jesus is already here. Where? In our spirit's capacity to know him and his great truth. The promise is now, not later.

The promise is in our headlights. It is our own focus we need to adjust.

Baggage

YEARS AGO, MY HUSBAND DROPPED ME, our two-year-old twins, our four-year-old son, and a pile of luggage at the airport's departure terminal. Then he went off to return the rental car. I thought he was going to deal with the baggage, and he thought I was going to deal with it. Neither of us did. At the baggage-claim carousel hours later in a different city, we waited for a very trusting and long time before realizing that our baggage was still on the curb in Orlando. Both of us did the best we could at the departure terminal. Our best did not include checking the luggage. A good self-knowing laugh made us realize that sometimes even our best is not good enough. We may be calm about our failures. We still fly home, baggage or not.

Calm means being free of anxiety and fear. Calm connects us but does not chain us to our baggage. Instead of attaching chains to our limbs, calm gives gossamer strings. A Yiddish proverb says that the only real problem is having nothing to carry.

Experienced travelers travel light. Jesus traveled so light that we never imagine him with so much as a backpack.

And yet his calm carries the world.

What are we carrying? What could we leave behind? Have we left something behind that we should return for? Is our husband or wife carrying too much of our family's load? By what grace could we carry more?

The calm of Christ carries all our questions along with us. That way, not one of them is too heavy.

Calm Manages
the Heavy Lifting

MANY OF US SUBSCRIBE TO THE FANTASY that if we just had the right equipment, we could manage our life. We buy gadgets and self-glorifications. We put on one new, expensive face and costume after another. But these external things rarely give us calm.

Calm comes from inside. It comes from what we can tap in our deep wells. Once we have tapped our deep wells, we find that magnificent security that says we belong to God, and God will never let us go. When we tap our deep wells, we find that we are able to carry a lot. We can even enjoy our different costumes more because we know they are not really "us" but simply costumes.

I learned something about equipment and gadgets and costumes on a strange journey years ago. I became acquainted with a ranger at the bottom of the Grand Canyon and discovered that the trails are littered daily with fancy hiking boots and other equipment. People can hike in with a lot of gear, but they can't hike out with it. Along our many paths, we may have to abandon some things that are too heavy or that pinch our feet. We may also have to lug them along with us. Whether lugging such stuff or leaving it behind, what matters is how we carry what we carry. Either way, calm can befriend us and get us home. When we are calm, we become light enough to fly or walk. Gossamer and grace manage what we can't. Calm carries the weight.

Tasks that seem so heavy on Tuesday can become light by Wednesday. Why? It depends on how we carry them out. If we tap our deep wells, we realize that our fancy hiking costume may not be as important (or heavy) as we thought it was. We are fine with it or without it.

Imagine that! We are fine.

Jesus reassures us from the inside out. This knowledge of who and Whose we are manages all the heavy lifting – the silly costume stuff and the big serious stuff, too – as it comes our way.

Calm Is a Promise of Renewal

GOD INTENDS GOOD THINGS FOR US. And still we find ourselves living without the depth of that promise. Pretty soon we will be making New Year's resolutions. The real go-getters have already started.

If you have ever wondered why New Year's resolutions are often joked about, wonder no more. Glenna Salsbury, in her book *The Art of the Fresh Start*, gets to the root of our perennial failure to become who we want to become. She says our resolutions are based in our fears and anxieties. Fear can't motivate us, and thus every time we even think of our resolution, we become more afraid.

What if we were to root our resolutions in God's promise of good things? What if we were to root them in our hopes and our calm?

From there we could become who we want to be.

Living in fear instead of hope, we are in good company: "For I do not do the good I want, but the evil I do not want is what I do." So said Saint Paul (Romans 7:19). Some live even more cynically: "Would that I didn't know now what I didn't know then." I found that on a coffee mug.

Human *being* is deep complexity. When we move to the place where we can just be – without becoming "better" – we can become, slowly and carefully, who we want to be.

I think of Elizabeth Barrett Browning, "All that I wanted to be and Am Not / Comforts Me." If we live in promise, we can keep resolutions. If we live in fear, we cannot.

The Calm of Clear Attention

CALM IS NOT SOMETHING WE CAN GET from beyond us. Its source is within us. Yes, God is Beyond us. *Big time!* But God comes to us through our insides, through the moments when we pay clear attention to who and what is really happening. God's route is inner despite the fact that God is outer and beyond and always a bit out of our reach. God comes to us in mysterious ways: when God is there, we simply "know" it. We go to deeper levels from a higher level. We don't control or summon God so much as we receive God's visits to us.

Clear attention and clear memory of these normal routings of the Holy Spirit are essential to those who would practice calm. We see God acting in and through us. We remember that God has acted in and through us and many other humans before now. We have faith — we know — that God will come to us if we but wait and see.

Calm is living at a deeper level than the ordinary. It is remembering our breath, our Source, our blood, our life.

We aren't just living: we are alive.

We may never have dramatic mystical experiences like those described by people such as William Wordsworth, Helen Keller, Saint Augustine, Ram Dass, or Petaga, a Sioux medicine man. But we can dare to be small mystics by simply paying lots of attention to what is going on here and now.

Some people may get overstimulated by paying lots of attention to everything. Susan Sontag, for example, once told an interviewer that she is not a very prolific writer simply because she is interested in so many things that she is undisciplined as a writer. "Maybe I have an Attention Surplus Disorder," Sontag said. "The easiest thing in the world for me is to pay attention."

That kind of stimulus bombardment is the opposite of calm. Calm calms when we pay enough attention that we get to the point of seeing what God is about in us and through us in any given moment or situation.

How do we practice the capacity for calm – for clearly attending to God's presence within us? One way is to spend a week doing one thing very carefully, like making breakfast or undressing, and then to conclude the week, Sabbath-like, with a meditation on what our attention taught us. The capacity to pay attention is recommended by both great mystics and ordinary people as a route to calm.

We pay enough attention so that we see not just our actions, or those of our companions, or even those of our historical moment. We pay enough attention to realize that God is at work within us, right here, right now.

Calm As Friends

M Y SEVENTH-GRADE SON TOLD ME, when I asked about his accelerated math test, "At least I wasn't nervous."

I asked who was. He described the girl sitting next to him. "She had to get up and go to the bathroom three times, her hands shaking the whole time, and she spent the whole test biting her pencil." This girl is eleven years old.

"Why weren't you nervous?" I asked my son.

He replied, "Because I have friends."

The connection between math and friendship, acceleration and accomplishment, performance and anxiety, are all part of God's toolbox. God uses friends to turn scarcity into plenty. God uses friends to turn anxiety into calm.

Remember when Mary visited Elizabeth, and Elizabeth and Mary's babies, even from the womb, knew their mothers' excitement at friendship? Remember when for you, being together with a good friend made all the fear go away? Surely that is why Mary made her journey to her friend: to calm her fear.

When community is not a part of people's lives, people embody their loneliness and anxiety. They drink too much. They get nervous. They become part of their own obstacle in developing the very community that could calm them.

Why is there so much substance abuse? One cause is the absence of community and the meaninglessness of many lives. I am not talking about the French existentialist Camus' good old-fashioned angst so much as our anxiety about "getting good grades," whether we are still in school or not. Performance preoccupies many of us. It is an obstacle to community and therefore to calm.

A tremendous paradox exists in today's human being. He or she is lazy – and works too hard. He or she is eager for ecstasy and meaning – and looks in all the wrong places for it. He or she is lonely – but operates as a unit in a kind of conformist horde.

Too many prayers ask God to "make me a money-making machine."

Instead we should pray for friends.

Calm As Prayer

TO BE ABLE TO PRAY, WE NEED SILENCE, sense, and spontaneity, according to liturgist Ruth Duck. She recommends several pointers for prayer. They include imagining and brainstorming, focusing and achieving a state of "flow," then stepping away and coming back to revise.

But who do we call God? How do we name God's name? Yes, God is the Creator and Preserver of us all. But is that all we can call God? Don't we need more?

No serious theologian claims that God is male. But lots of people can't pray to a God without gender. Such prayer is too impersonal.

I often image God as an old woman fumbling for her keys in a parking lot. I think of God as more like us than not. I don't believe God is all-powerful. I hope I'm wrong. I just can't imagine a big sky God. An earthier God warms me more.

How do I pray? Like Ruth Duck says: In imagination and brainstorming, focus and flow – and then in long silence, coming back to revise.

She is talking more about public prayer than private prayer. But her ideas also work for the prayers of our inner heart. There is nothing wrong with getting things right in prayer, nothing wrong with getting to the right words for the right thought, even and especially before God.

We can also pray like the Hebrews – by breathing, by silence, by sense, by spontaneity, by the waiting Ruth Duck recommends, by stepping away to reflect, by waiting to find the right name for our God. That name will proba-bly even change over time or prayer by prayer.

A long time ago, I wrote a poem. It began: "God, I cannot call you Father . . ."

It ended:
"But still you call me Daughter."

What we call God matters less than the fact that God calls us.

find out who God is for you. Name God. You'll be on the first step to prayer.

And prayer will bring you calm. It will make sure, as Rick Hamlin, a writer and editor at *Guideposts* puts it, that you have a quiet room in the back of your mind, a room of your own, a place you can go.

A place of calm repose.

Calm As Inclusion

I N THE EPISCOPAL PRAYER BOOK, WE ARE
taught to pray for "all sorts and conditions"
of people. This phrase is a wonderful catchall
of life's experience, both inner and outer. We
are so many different things all at once. Some
of us are poor materially and rich spiritually;
others are the reverse. Still others are poor both
ways. A rare few are rich both ways.

Some of us are Zenny. In a recent, very
inclusive book about Zen, Bernard Glassman
encourages us to eat as a way of knowing God.
Glassman tells us that Zen is the art of eating
the supreme meal, that we may prepare this
meal for ourselves both in our kitchen and
outside of it, that nothing should be wasted,
that all should be savored, and that good food
comes from the right mixture in life and at the
table.

Eucharist is at the heart of Zen, which is another way of reminding us of all sorts and conditions.

Bernard Glassman is an unusually interesting person. Raised Jewish and attracted at an early age to the teachings of a thirteenth-century Japanese monk, Dogen Zenji, Glassman is now a highly regarded Zen master, or *roshi*. He has taken his large spirit to poor people by celebrating an open street seder for homeless men in New York City's Bowery. He is also one of the founders of a profitable bakery in Yonkers, New York. The bakery is an economic development project that employs and trains poor people. He has just begun a ministry to persons with HIV and AIDS as well.

His witness is not just social or economic. It is also personal and meditative: "Use what you have." "Throw nothing away." "Recognize your faults as your best ingredients." "Be inclusive of all sorts and conditions."

Life has at least five main courses to Glassman: spirituality, study, livelihood, social action, and relationship and community. The art of living involves a good mix of these five ingredients.

Roshi Glassman is a spiritual leader of the White Plum Sangha and abbot of the Zen Community of New York and the Zen Center of Los Angeles. He is also an aeronautical engineer, an entrepreneur, and a social activist who founded the Greyston Mandala, a group of social service organizations in Yonkers, New York.

For all sorts and conditions of people! Amen.

Zenny Calm

IF YOU ARE ONE OF THE MANY PEOPLE WHO find yourself using the made-up word Zenny from time to time, you have already understood the matter of understanding God. God behaves in wild ways. God combines things that are not normally combined well, like social action and meditation, or eating well and living spiritually. Like virginity and pregnancy, or death and new life. Like a few loaves and fishes having the capacity to feed five thousand people. Or babies carrying divinity. Or heaven becoming earth. Or God becoming human.

What Christians call the Incarnation is a strange but intentional combination of word and flesh. God wasn't happy just being "up" in heaven; God came down to earth.

God's goodness is weird. God's goodness combines what others wouldn't dare.

It may also be possible to combine anxiety and calm. We can't live anxiety-free. If we became stress-free, we would not be very human. Plus we would have to live our life blind to what is going on in the world: the world is scary and deep. People get hurt on highways and in tenements; not to be anxious about these sorts of things would be not to see.

We who dare see, see deeply. We see that beneath the anxiety that accompanies our days there is God's deep peace. A Silent and Holy Night. A deeper calm. One that anchors people amid freak accidents, one that warms mothers who don't know where their children's next supper will come from.

God combines oil with water in a Zenny way. God combines hope with despair. God does these things on purpose because God is intentionally with us, as in Messiah, God-with-us.

How Much Calm Is Enough?

WE NEED TO "RIGHTSIZE" THE ADVENT promises – not downsize but right-size them.

If "all is calm," does that mean that every-thing, all the time, is calm? I think not. That would put Adrenalin out of business.

I frequently put too much baking powder in cookie recipes. I don't mean to trivialize the matter of scale by the comparison but to acknowledge the utter simplicity of going too far, of using too much. Excess is almost ordi-nary in our society. We invented the concept of "All-You-Can-Eat."

A little bit of baking powder goes a long way. A little bit of calm goes a long way.

If we could be sure that we knew how to experience calm some of the time on a regular basis, we could imagine salvation. We could remember what we know regularly, which is that Jesus Christ has saved and secured us. We don't need to know it every minute to know it. We need to know that we can know it when we need to know it – like in a long line waiting for a ferry we may not make, or when waiting for the results of our cancer test or our child's cancer test. We need to know that we can know God when we need to know God.

Then we will have enough calm to understand that *all*, at its depth, *is* calm.

Calm As a Consumer

WAL-MART IS ABOUT TO MOVE INTO my backyard. Instead of smelling manure being distributed on a field, I will be smelling the temptation of low prices made possible by cheap labor.

Wal-Mart uses cheap labor from India, Indonesia, China, Mexico, and beyond to make its products. I have a friend who shops the world for the cheapest, cutest baskets. She then sells them to Wal-Mart. I buy them. The people who make them are often fourteen years old or even younger. They get a penny a basket; Wal-Mart gets $9.99. At a ratio of one thousand pennies to one, that is a pretty good profit. One would imagine that Wal-Mart could afford to be a union shop.

How can I becalm myself as a consumer while knowing that I am benefiting at the expense of child labor? Is there any calm in my becoming like Bill Gates, who is estimated to be worth more personally than the hundred million poorest Americans combined? Is my goal to become Godzilla? Do American consumers have a choice other than becoming like a long-unnoticed tick on a dog?

I could, in an act of middle-class resistance, choose not to shop at Wal-Mart. But I'll bet Wal-Mart will get money from me before it is all over. Even if I hold out, I'll bet my three teenagers will get there.

So how do I stay sane and calm while Wal-Mart waltzes into town? What are the layers of life that keep trying to get calm but can't because they are riddled with impossibilities? In this economy I can't buy "well." I can't be calm as a consumer.

One friend told me she is not fighting Wal-Mart because "Kmart is right across the street, doing the same thing." Another excused herself by saying, "Face it — you are rich in the scheme of things. Just enjoy it." Another thought it was elitist to fight against low prices. Still another said she didn't have time to fight gross largeness because she was working three jobs to support her four children in college. Still another thought that Wal-Mart would win even if people sued, even if people committed guerilla warfare. Yet another thought that building a Wal-Mart was a good use of a neglected space.

One day my thirteen-year-old daughter and one of her friends sat in the backseat of my car. The friend said, "I love living in Amherst. It's the only place I know where the local McDonalds went out of business."

I couldn't help myself. I asked her what she liked about that fact. "It means we're different. It means we're special."

So all my friends and this girl are right. But the girl is right only because Amherst has Hadley next door to set it apart. It is worthless, elitist, silly, and a waste of precious time to fight Wal-Mart. It is only possible to live in consumer calm some other way — like in a mythical theory of exceptionalism.

In a world riddled with economic impossibility, we live in a mythic and fictional calm. But at least it is calm. We use the idea of particularity to imagine our way out of the truth, which is that Amherst and Hadley look a lot like Leominster or Pittsburgh or Orlando. We imagine ourselves as different while sneaking across the border to buy a basket or two.

Other myths assuage savage choices. We say we are happy enough to care for the poor in our own backyard but not the poor in Indonesia, even though Indonesian poor are moving into our backyard. The myth of the backyard and the myth of exceptionalism are roommates in most Amherst homes.

The myth of the backyard is that our paychecks come from someone we know, and that our mortgages, car payments, and insurance are going to someone who looks a lot like Mister Rogers. The myth is convenient, widely accepted, and completely false. It is economic fiction, not fact.

Neither the source nor the destination of our money is local. Banks and mortgages are national, if not global. Insurance companies conglomerate at a rate close to that of banks. Wal-Mart will help make obsolete many local businesses that really grew up in our backyard.

The real bargains are not at Wal-Mart. The real bargains are in mythic ideas that we buy for nothing. But we get what we pay for.

The Dow is not the Tao. Economic globalization is not inevitable: it is, however, very real. And globalization is evident in my backyard and my pocketbook, right next to my charge card, as well in the shoes on the feet under my table. Indonesia is my backyard. It is a place as special and exceptional as Amherst. That is not a fiction; that is a fact. And it is in that reality that I need to seek my calm as a consumer.

Sometimes We Just Have to Get Out of Our Own Way

A FRIEND ONCE TOLD ME A STORY ABOUT the famous Reformation theologians Calvin and Zwingli. The time was the sixteenth century; the place, Europe. They were part of the group that gave birth to a new branching in Christianity, that of Protestantism. They were serious about their mission to break away from Roman Catholicism.

I have no such heroic mission in life, but I do find lots of small and large conflicts in the churches I serve. This story helps me find a calm way through conflict.

In the story these two important figures are on their way to a major confrontation over the directions of their separate movements. They are to visit the very next day. The night before the visit, Zwingli dreams that two goats are circling two mountains. Ambling. Walking in a deep calm. All of a sudden it becomes apparent that their paths are not only going to cross but that they are going to cross at a stretch in the mountain where the pass is narrow and only one will be able to go at a time.

The goats continue on their way and, sure enough, they meet.

One goat lies down and allows the other to walk through the pass, then gets up and continues on the journey. The passing goat could easily have stepped on the goat that had lain down, but it did not. The goat that had yielded was not injured in any way.

Zwingli wondered for the rest of his life why, with his God's-eye view of the goat's passage, he never learned which goat represented him.

This parable has helped me on more than one occasion. Sometimes if I remember how large the world is – and stay away from the narrowness of my own violence – I see that there is more than one way to cross a mountain.

Calm waits with me when I wait for others to pass.

Calm Waits for the Truth

CALM SLOWS THINGS DOWN SO WE CAN
speak from our depth instead of our
surface. When we speak from our surface, or
for the crowd, or for the quick fix, we speak
weakly. We do not speak from our strength.
We don't give ourselves time to really see and
understand what is happening. We rush to judgments – and these judgments are often falsely
colored by prejudice or wishful thinking.

E. M. Forster's *A Passage to India* is a famous
story about an Englishwoman who accuses a
Muslim man of attacking her in a cave. It is a
remarkable treatment of how racism works
through manners as well as economics and pol-
itics. The woman was not attacked, but she so
feared she might be that she imagined that it
actually happened. Our reactions on the surface
of communications often originate in these

kinds of misperceptions and faulty expectations. Because our husband hurt us once by not liking a certain kind of food, we do a protective reaction strike whenever we serve something like it. Because our boss is always mean right before school vacations, we imagine she is being mean sometimes even when she is not. We protect ourselves rather than calm ourselves.

Calm is the permission to take our time to see what is really going on. When the Englishwoman accuses a Muslim Indian of attacking her in a cave, and then tries to repent her accusation, she causes a great frenzy. We all know how big the fuss can become when falsehoods are put into play. Lives are ruined. In the novel the Muslim man imagines his life is ruined, even though, finally, it is not. The woman's life is in fact ruined by her foolish, confused falsehood: she no longer trusts herself or her judgment. The point of calm truth-seeking and calm truth-speaking is to ruin as few lives as possible – and to open the pathways for confession, forgiveness, restoration, and a glimpse of truth.

It is often as good to refrain from speaking as it is to speak: in silence we allow room for the calm that can help us sort out difficult, confusing moments and interactions.

Lots of things are much more than they appear. Many things are genuinely confusing. They are not made less confusing by quick words or quick judgments. We need to slow down our perceptions and look carefully and calmly. Did my husband really mean that cruel thing I thought he said? What if he did? What if he didn't? Do I need to respond now or can I wait until I have re-established self-control?

Even if we can attain just a little calm, it is often enough to allow us the time and inclination to become more deeply calm, calm enough to deal with life's bigger difficulties. "Slow down" is never bad advice. Small calm waits for large calm to develop.

Shakespeare gave similar advice to kings when he wrote:

> Time's glory is to calm contending kings,
> To unmask falsehood, and bring truth to light.

Calm waits for the truth. Calm also creates the capacity for truth within us: when we slow down, and calm down, we can see clearly enough to perceive what is really going on.

Slowing down to achieve calm, rightly understood, is a time-saver, not a time-waster. When all is said and done, calm causes our relationships to be much less troubled and diminishes our confusion. Anxiety wastes time; calm guards it.

Calm Families

MAGGIE SCARF, A LEADING WRITER ON families and relationships, writes about family typologies. She says there are at least five typologies: critical, confirming, endorsing, adoring, and neglecting.

She also says that we become the kind of parents we have.

Most of us begin our life as parents by utterly rejecting this obvious fact. We are going to be so much better than our parents that it isn't even funny. In fact, it is very funny. Our efforts to best our own parents utterly fail.

Trying to best our parents is a horrible thing to do. The weight alone could kill us. Appreciating our parents and appreciating ourselves, on the other hand, is a gift.

The first of these patterns turns us toward a heavy darkness. The second turns us toward light.

The source of lightness here for me has been to learn to love my mother as my mother – she will never be exactly the kind of mother I would have hoped for. I want this grace, too, from my children – and I suspect the only way I will get it, or deserve it, is to have it myself.

My mother did the very best she could, just as I am doing the best I can right now. Neither is perfect. Sometimes when I realize what she was up against, I give up on the occasional practice, while driving to work, of trying to explain, or more likely rationalize, to myself the real reasons our family breakfast was such a disaster.

To get back for a moment to Maggie Scarf's family typologies: My husband was parented critical and he parents critical. I was parented neglected and adoring, on alternate Tuesdays, and I parent the same. My hopes to best my parents have met with failure.

Our early teenagers ("Why can't I get Mortal Kombat?") have given us lots of opportunities to demonstrate how our parents parented us. It is as if we are a daily taped recording.

Someday I hope to title a book *Good but Not Perfect Mothers*. Imperfection is not the only destiny I have left in this vocation of motherhood. I can at least hope to be good.

What would a calm family be? Calm and critical. Calm and adoring. Calm and neglecting. Do you see the difference? We add salvation to our family's pattern and we become a bit more the people we had hoped to become – not people better than our parents but people a bit more like Jesus.

Calm Quits and Revives

ONE WOMAN HAD SPENT THREE CHRIST-mases in jail. Her son was six years old when she arrived; he was nine the day he ran down the hall to leap into his mother's arms during the visiting hours. The guard stopped him. "No running in the jail." The mother slapped the guard. She lost her visit that day.

Later she went to the guard and apologized for breaking the rule. With tears in his eyes, the guard apologized for keeping the rule.

Because of his apology to her, she was able to ask his help. Could he do something to stop the dirty talking from the staff lounge that traveled through the jail's vents and imposed itself on the inmates? She didn't want to be forced to hear it anymore. He stopped it.

At first all calm had left her. But then it returned. She found a way when there was no way. The way was her capacity to apologize. It revived her calm.

One Easter Sunday the truly excellent jail choir's organist gave the Christian hug of peace to one of the women inmates as she arrived, joyously, for services. We lost our organist for the morning service. "No hugging allowed."

Calm quit. Then calm revived.

Naturally God intervened and found a way for singing and music that day. God found a way where there was no way. (That statement of faith is one we all hear often in the jail.)

One of the inmates stood up and said, "I can lead a song." She was quick to add a disclaimer: "But I can't lead any religious stuff." We asked her what she could lead us in singing. "I Believe That Children Have a Future." We gasped. Next to the Resurrection, or the hope of life after death or jail, mentioning children in the jail is a sure three-hanky experience.

Our volunteer Easter choir gave a magnificent rendition of the popular song guaranteeing children a future. The choir was joined by all fifty of the women who were at worship that morning in loud, exuberant singing.

After the Easter service, one of the women asked if she could have a bud from one of the lilies. Within seconds all the other inmates had come forward with a similar request. Soon the naked lilies stood on the altar. Now every time I see an altar filled with flowers, I remember those naked plucked Easter lilies!

Calm quits. Then calm returns. You can count on it.

Calm Near, Calm Far Away

GERMAN THEOLOGIAN KARL BARTH argued that our language about God should begin with language about Christ. For Hispanics the Incarnation exemplifies the ultimate *mestizaje*, the juncture of divinity and humanity.

Christmas is the calm of Christ come down to earth. How quietly. How quietly.

Both Germans and American Hispanics argue for Christ in a way that religious universalists do not — they want a God up close and personal. That's what Christmas gives us.

According to theologian Orlando Costas, the Incarnation forces us to see God's activity within the context of history. This prevents us from turning God into an abstract being removed from human experience.

Unfortunately North American Protestants have been more than capable of turning God into a static and abstract notion removed from the immediacy of human experience.

Many of us find the closeness of God the opposite of calming. The very intimacy of God-with-Us, Emmanuel, makes us nervous. We might echo the sentiment of this line from the work of the poet Rainer Maria Rilke: "Who is this Christ, who interferes in everything?"

This matter of God being both close and far away, this matter of God showing up on earth, is not easy to understand. The poet Kathleen Norris has said that as she grew in her understanding of Christianity she could grasp most everything about it except Christ. "I often felt a void at the heart of things. My Christianity seemed to be missing its center."

Norris discovered a concrete image that helped her gain a deeper understanding of the Trinity. It is an image that can also help us see how God can be both very near and very far away.

Tertullian, a curmudgeonly theologian of the early church, provided the metaphor that brought Norris's understanding home. "It's an image of the Trinity as a plant, with the Father as a deep root, the Son as the shoot that breaks forth into the world, and the Spirit as that which spreads beauty and fragrance."

When God comes close, we need not be afraid. See the beauty, breathe deep the fragrance.

Calm Is Focus

THE BIGGEST THING THAT HAPPENED around here last year was the new deck on the back of our old house. The deck itself is inconsequential – but what it represents is not. A heavy snow on April first (!) last year, the day after Easter, knocked down the old deck. Crash. The insurance people said we were entitled to collect three thousand dollars or so to repair what was clearly a six-thousand-dollar project. For months we wrung our hands. What to do? We looked all spring at the mess of ancient wisteria wound around rotted poles, yellow rose bushes unable to make their annual climb for want of a hand up. It was a sad-looking and anxiety-provoking scene.

All of a sudden the idea came: the new deck could easily be half the size of the old deck. Also half the price. Our trusty contractor agreed and designed a new deck that snuggles the back of the house as though it were part of the original design. People stop to ask who built it, so nicely does it fit. And we have a morality play in our backyard: downsizing, designed well and carried out with intelligence, may be the best thing to do in the year one turns fifty.

Downsizing, at its best, can give us the right size. It gives us focus. Once we know the proper size of a thing, we know what to add and what to subtract. We know how to move from frenzy and hurry to calm and an easy, human pace.

Rilke wrote about something else focus can bring. He advises us to "gain the confidence of those whom others think poor." His words remake the Advent promise that valleys will be lifted up and mountains made low (see Isaiah 40:3–4). The best things I do are in the valley, on the edge, in the parking lot after the meeting, with those who are displaced and ignored by the system. The worst I can do is to hallow the mountains, to try to becalm myself by seeking that which is bigger and better and more mountainous.

The valleys are the action. Small is plenty. With decks. With people. There really is enough.

I heard someone say that the Hubble telescope is a parable about size. Supposedly if you take a grain of sand for each star you can see in the sky, the sand will fit into a cup. If you take a grain of sand for every star in the Milky Way, you will fill up a big bowl. If you take a grain of sand for every star visible through the Hubble telescope, you will need all the sand in the world, from every beach, to be sure that every star is accounted for.

So don't worry too much about anything. Count the stars from your small place in the valley. Focus on the small. Focus on the little. And treasure the calm that resides in the small!

Calm Is Tuning

YOU KNOW HOW BADLY UNTUNED
instruments can sound when played by
untuned people. You also know how good the
opposite can be.

We will sing a lot of Christmas carols this
season. They will calm us in a way that almost
nothing else can.

They will save us from the "Relentlessly
Quaint Parts of Christmas," as one pessimist
put it. We can also tune ourselves by decorating
less and lighting more candles. Or singing a
simple, "Jingle hell, jingle hell, jingle less the
way" just to get out the venom that builds up
as the season becomes increasingly commer-
cially disrespected.

Some feel dread about Christmas. When
we do, we should tune ourselves differently,
maybe even protect ourselves from a little glitz

and glitter on behalf of a little quiet and soul saving.

There is what Robert Pinsky calls a pendulum to expectation. What is a pendulum when it comes to expectation? It is the certainty that there will be rhythm. It is the way we change, almost constantly. Nothing much stays the same. The fact that we are unstable is our stability. The fact that we change is our foundation. Our rock is the way we move, or hold ourselves, while the pendulum swings.

We tune ourselves to movement. We tune ourselves as movement.

The issue is how to hear angels above the din of the modern mania. We need both to tune and to train ourselves for calm.

Calm Is Fragments

L ET ME TELL YOU A STORY ABOUT OLD
First Church in Springfield, Massachusetts,
and an astonishing mission it has in Nicaragua.

The "Pilgrim Ladies" of this parish meet
weekly to unpack boxes filled with prosthetic
legs, arms, fingers, and hands. These used items
are the gift of people who have died but whose
limbs didn't; they are given by their loved ones
because "it is very hard to throw things like
these away."

The youth group of the parish then unfas-
tens the screws and fasteners that were custom
designed to the size of the original owner.
Next, the pastor and several of his old friends
pack the material in duffel bags and deliver
them to mission sites in Nicaragua.

I have seen photos from the trips to Nicaragua, and they are unbelievable – especially

the scenes of the duffel bags being opened for inspection at customs.

In Nicaragua, specially trained Nicaraguan surgeons attach and refasten the prosthetic devices. They help people who have been hurt by land mines and in other kinds of accidents to build new lives via new limbs.

This is one of the most simple mission projects I have ever heard of – and it happens with almost no money exchanging hands. As life and time go on, more people around the country hear about the project, and more "stuff" arrives in the mail at Old first Church.

These recycled devices, artificial parts that make human beings complete, remind me of nothing so much as the fragmented body of Christ: here we have an experience of broken bodies and blood poured out that involves ordinary people in extraordinary ways.

Calm comes in little pieces as well. None of us lives without injury to our capacity for calm. We have internalized lots of stress and lots of anxiety. But we all live with the capacity for calm as well. Each of us has a good chunk of bread or truth; we have places where we go deep and from which we can help others.

When we put all these things into duffel bags and exchange them, when we give what we have and receive what we need, calm unifies.

Community yields calm in a way that one individual all alone probably cannot. We are all partial. We are all fragments. We are all injured.

And we are all complete.

In the unity of Christ, who came at Christmas to restore an original unity to the world, we are complete. And in that completeness, we are calm.

Calm Is Magnification

WHEN MARY TALKS ABOUT HER SOUL magnifying the Lord, she means it. The Lord got big. Mary got big. How do *we* enlarge?

We enlarge by seeing a lot in a little.

Remember the famous lines of William Blake?

> To see a world in a grain of sand
> And a heaven in a wild flower
> Hold infinity in the palm of your hand
> And eternity in an hour.

Blake knew that a large reality can be contained in a small space. There is a world in a tiny particle of sand; an hour of a life can define a lifetime.

It is one thing to *see* a lot in a little. It is another thing to take that way of perceiving and turn it into a concrete reality.

But one single person, or a small number of people, can have an impact on the world at large. Think of the scientist who works alone, discovers the polio vaccine, and removes that great fear from all our lives. Or the "radical" thinkers who brought child labor in the United States virtually to an end, and those who continue that work throughout the world. Or the poet who writes about seeing the world in a grain of sand, and enables generations of readers to understand life in a new and inspired way.

God did the same sort of thing. God took one true human and saved the whole world with that One. God used a little to accomplish a lot.

We can do the same.

Calm After Clutter

HAVE YOU EVER NOTICED THE WAY FLIGHT attendants prepare a cabin for landing? They approach the job almost like a familiar ritual. With, it seems, very little effort or emotion, they gather trash and trays, cups and clutter, deposit it all behind a special door, and sit down in the special seat that faces the passengers. They are done with their job, and wait, calmly, for the airplane to land.

Now think about the way we pick up the house the day after Christmas. Everywhere there is mess: ridiculous numbers of items and packages need to find a place. New things need to be put away. Old things need to be recycled. Leftover food fills up every corner. If children are around, they have already made their new toys look old and comfy. To say that the house is usually a mess, like the airplane after a long flight, is not to exaggerate.

Some people find it hard to be calm in these kinds of situations. The mess robs us of peace. Clutter confronts us with tough questions, like where did all this stuff come from and who needs it anyway? Other people, like flight attendants, just go through the ritual of picking up, cleaning up, checking seatbelts, straightening seats. As we watch, we sense their calm.

Great rituals are part of everyday living, and one of them is "picking up." Instead of being afraid of or unnerved by the restoration of order, we might enjoy the process. We might see it as saying good-bye to the old and hello to the new. We might understand cleaning in a spiritual way, as preparing the way for a new self.

Lots of the gifts we get are actually new costumes. When we put them on, we also put on a new role. The same is true of the way we grow, spiritually, toward calm. We are trying on a new self. We are taking off the old and putting on the new.

Clutter, whether the day after a big holiday or after a flight — or just after a long day when everyone has been at work — is a fact of life. We can be scared of it or we can embrace it. We can embrace it calmly.

Traveling Light
in the Grand Canyon

THERE WE WERE, TWO TWENTY-EIGHT-
year-olds in love, on the rim of the Grand
Canyon on New Year's Eve, watching the sun
go down and realizing that the hotel really
was full. Even if it wasn't, we couldn't have
afforded to sleep there. But in the first years of
that first marriage, we tended to take one problem at a time. My husband had a brainstorm.
"I'll bet the ranger in the bottom of the canyon is lonely, especially tonight. Let's call him
and see how he would feel about some guests."
The idea had merit: its desperation matched
our own.

The ranger's telephone number was right in
the book. We dialed, explained our situation,
and offered a barter of groceries packed down.

Gary, the ranger, said that actually he and his most pregnant wife, Gina, would love company and would especially enjoy company that brought guacamole and tortilla chips. Gina took the phone from Gary and let us know that she concurred.

The hardest part of the evening was finding avocados at six p.m. We did find them and didn't mind paying the rather astronomical price. A half hour after dusk we were on our way down. No packs, except the groceries.

Whatever hatred I have since developed for luggage must have originated that night. The freedom of moving without carrying! The beauty of the canyon unobstructed by plans to see it! Gina had insisted on the phone that we bring *nothing* but the chips and dips. She kept saying, "We have everything."

Little did we know. After a light but uneventful passage down the curving canyon, we arrived at the bottom. It was warmer by twenty degrees in the canyon. We had gone down so quickly that we passed by the ranger's house and went as close to the Colorado River as we could get. There on that hot, grassy plain we looked up and saw several caribou, like statues, preparing for their own version of "Auld Lang

Syne." One coyote actually seemed to be singing it!

As we retraced our steps to the ranger's house, we had an attack of shyness. Surely this was the right place; there was no other building anywhere. But what if these people were serial killers? Or strange in some other way? What would we do then? Call the park ranger?

What some people see as adventure, others see as stress. The reverse is also true. The stress that night enhanced the adventure. By the time we knocked on the door, we were almost disappointed to be greeted by such normal people!

They were both about our age. Gina was eight, maybe twelve months pregnant. They were dressed casually. They let us in to their large cabin and served us a nice dinner. Then we played games. They apparently had every board game, pool table, and entertainment device in the world. The games gave us a chance to get to know one another. If we had been older, perhaps in our forties, we probably would have sat there interminably having "conversation." After a while we were gamed out.

Then they showed us their "sports room." It was full of abandoned sports equipment.

High-class hiking boots. Expensive backpacks. Fancy hats. Fancier walking sticks. Three-hundred-dollar goose-down vests. "People can walk in easily enough with all this stuff; they just can't walk out. That's why I told you not to bring any more stuff. I wanted to make sure you could walk out."

The next morning – which came around noon – Gina served her famous pancakes. Thin buckwheats, spread with cottage cheese alternated with orange marmalade, stacked seven high and sliced to show the stripe. "These are guaranteed to get you all the way out from here. I've done it many times." She walked us halfway up the rim and pointed out a shortcut. We did one more verse of "Auld Lang Syne" together and said good-bye.

That night was a lesson in packing light. A lesson in not overarranging. A lesson about youth: walking in *is* a lot easier than walking out! Should other old acquaintances be forgot, well, that's all right. But not these.

Gina and Gary, and all that stuff, taught us, among other things, the calm that resides just the other side of there being no room for us in the inn.

Calm in Trouble

BY ALL RIGHTS, THE FIRST CHRISTMAS EVE was a very dramatic night. A baby being born in an unprepared place, without help. Crowded quarters. Lots of travelers in a time when travel was probably much less easy than it is now. No phones, no fax, no doctors, no birthing rooms.

There was good reason for people to panic that night. But they did not panic. They waited for and on God, and God did not disappoint.

When we get into genuinely scary circumstances, surely we should call for help. Or fax for help. Or call on professionals like police or doctors or lawyers or all three. And we should do one thing more: we should wait on and for God.

God is an experienced emergency worker. I'll never forget a parishioner telling me once that when he had his heart attack, the God he "didn't believe in" accompanied him in the helicopter to the hospital.

The God we sometimes don't believe in will also be with us when we are in trouble. God is good at crisis. God may even prefer Christmas Eve drama to regular Sunday worship. (Not that there is anything inferior about regular summoning of the Holy. Rather, we need to remember that crisis summons the Holy all by itself.)

I remember going to a doctor in France once with a sick child. The doctor treated the kid on the spot, with no nurse, no receptionist, no urgent-care hotline phone, no insurance papers. When the examination was done, the doctor asked for money. I handed it to him. He put it in his pocket. I found the simplicity of the entire affair to be magnificent. The order of the exchange had an appropriateness that was quite beautiful.

My baby had a problem. The doctor solved it. I was scared stiff. But I didn't need to be scared. God was nigh.

Dr. David Hilfiker, in his book *Not All of Us Are Saints*, tells story after story of his work with the poor and the sick in Washington, D.C. He says that the thing that amazed him most of all about these people was the degree to which they had internalized their abandonment and poverty. Children who had not been adequately loved now saw themselves as unlovable; young people who had been inadequately trusted could not trust; people who were materially poor could no longer even imagine a different sort of life.

Christmas Eve, however, is a time when we remember that we have been given the opposite experience of abandonment: God is nigh. God, who could have abandoned creation, does not. God "comes down" and gets close.

What if we were to internalize God's presence?

Calm Is the Christmas Point of View

What if we saw the world as though Bethlehem were the town we were born in? We would stand in awe at the edge of the manger and give thanks for all that we saw. The baby. The effect of the baby on the people of the town. The effect of the baby on the parents. The bright star. The sigh of relief of the many who had waited too long for the Messiah and half hoped and half feared that he might have come.

The shepherds had waited forever, slowly, calmly in a field. The Magi got excited: they were out there looking, standing on tiptoes, getting ready for the big calm of the Messiah.

How do we see with the eyes of Christmas? Surrounded by the heavenly host, we would no longer fear for the poor. Or for ourselves. We would know that we are all protected and that the angels are steadily filling the hungry with good things.

A Honduran refugee once challenged me with these words: "Why do you lose your hope when we have not lost ours?" She was talking about my fear that the poor would never be safe in this world. They *are* safe. Messiah has come.

Our wombs leap with joy, as in Luke 1:44. Like Mary, we carry a huge load, joyously. How do pregnant women ever get through pregnancy? So much is always going on. But they live their lives "regularly." Just like this, regularly, we may wait for the Messiah to come again: we go about our business, all the while knowing that we are accompanied by a miracle.

Eugene Petersen has a poem in which he calls this leap in the womb a dance to "world beat of the womb's music." Messiah comes in great rhythms. Calm and slow rhythms, the ones the shepherds heard. And with rhythms of excitement, which caught the ears of the Magi.

And surely, like in pregnancy, all of a sudden things aren't calm at all. Birth of the many children of Bethlehem, born year in and year out, and then, lo and behold, Christ is born.

Christ is born.

After the loud joy of our Bethlehem-self would come the silent joy. We would have a new way of keeping silence, a deeper calm. "How Silently," we would sing.

We would have new understandings of the words *long expected*.

What in our own life is long expected? For what are we still waiting? Is it possible that all we have waited for and are waiting for is already here?

That calm is Christ, and Christ is calm now that our Christ has come.

Beat in our heart and soul and womb, O God. Beat out the rhythm of calm and safety and salvation. Let us all hear the beat together. Amen.

Go to Bethlehem

L ET US GO NOW TO BETHLEHEM AND SEE *this thing that has taken place"* (Luke 2:15). Place our hopes on Bethlehem this season, O God. Convince us that small is victor over large, that we can find a lot in a little. Slow us down. Move us out of the fast lane. Let every plan we make contain the seed of your Son's birth so that when the silent night comes, we can know the song in its silence, the gift in giving gifts, and the peace that passes understanding in the quiet of our hearts.

Let us go to Bethlehem to find him who brings the scattered home. Come softly to us in this season, O Jesus. Bring us home by your path. Open our eyes and ears that we may welcome the life you bring. Revive the desert places in us that we may yet blossom.

Let us go to Bethlehem to meet him who hears us when we have no words, no justifications, no excuses, only the thud of facts and gnawing memories, only the knowledge that too many tables are thinly laid and that we, too, are poor in ways that frighten us.

Let us go to Bethlehem to find the child who amazes us. Bethlehem — so small, so insignificant — it seems unlikely that you should use it for your grand purpose. But you sneak in there, Holy Child, so silently, almost unobserved. And if you can use Bethlehem, that means you can use us. Come into our quiet space and point us to the purposes you have for us. At your manger make sense of our lives.

Let us go to Bethlehem and see that our usual hopes are too small, that the pragmatism of this world is inadequate to grasp the things you have in mind. Make us wild in hope — that AIDS will be cured, that peace will blanket the earth, that we will find calm for our souls. Show us that we are not alone, that you are with us, that in your smallness we find all we truly need.